MIDLOTHIAN PUBLIC LIBRARY

3 1614 00206 2439

W9-AOA-095

Step by Step

The Story of Salt

It Starts with the Sea

MIDLOTHIAN PUBLIC LIBRARY
14701 S. KENTON AVENUE
MIDLOTHIAN, IL 60445

Lisa Owings

Lerner Publications ◆ Minneapolis

JUV NON FIC 664.4 OWI

Copyright © 2021 by Lerner Publishing Group, Inc.

All rights reserved. International copyright secured. No part of this book may be reproduced, stored in a retrieval system, or transmitted in any form or by any means—electronic, mechanical, photocopying, recording, or otherwise—without the prior written permission of Lerner Publishing Group, Inc., except for the inclusion of brief quotations in an acknowledged review.

Lerner Publications Company
An imprint of Lerner Publishing Group, Inc.
241 First Avenue North
Minneapolis, MN 55401 USA

For reading levels and more information, look up this title at www.lernerbooks.com.

Image credits: @Michi B./Moment/Getty Images, p. 3; Malcolm MacGregor/Moment/Getty Images, pp. 5, 23 (sea); Federica Grassi/Moment Open/Getty Images, p. 7; David Toussaint/Moment Open/Getty Images, pp. 9, 23 (crystals); iStock/Getty Images, p. 11; IHervas/iStock/Getty Images, p. 13; Patrick BOX/Gamma-Rapho/Getty Images, pp. 15, 23 (factory); John Carey/Photolibrary/Getty Images, p. 17; JEAN-CHRISTOPHE VERHAEGEN/AFP/Getty Images, pp. 19. 23 (machines); Richard Levine/Alamy Stock Photo, p. 21; Image Source/Stockbyte/Getty Images, p. 22. Cover: Tainar/iStock/Getty Images (water); t_kimura/E+/Getty Images (salt).

Main body text set in Mikado a Medium.
Typeface provided by HVD Fonts.

Editor: Alison Lorenz

Library of Congress Cataloging-in-Publication Data

Names: Owings, Lisa, author.
Title: The story of salt : it starts with the sea / Lisa Owings.
Description: Minneapolis : Lerner Publications, 2021 | Series: Step by step | Includes bibliographical references and index. | Audience: Ages 4-8 | Audience: Grades K-1 | Summary: "How does salt go from the sea to flavoring your food? Straightforward text and engaging photos help readers find out" —Provided by publisher.
Identifiers: LCCN 2019045751 (print) | LCCN 2019045752 (ebook) | ISBN 9781541597259 (library binding) | ISBN 9781728401164 (ebook)
Subjects: LCSH: Salt—Juvenile literature. | Salt industry and trade—Juvenile literature.
Classification: LCC TN900 .O95 2021 (print) | LCC TN900 (ebook) | DDC 664.4—dc23

LC record available at https://lccn.loc.gov/2019045751
LC ebook record available at https://lccn.loc.gov/2019045752

Manufactured in the United States of America
1-47829-48269-12/18/2019

Salt flavors our food!

How is salt made?

Salt comes from
the sea.

The seawater is
pumped into ponds.

Salt crystals form.

Workers gather
the salt.

Trucks take the
salt to a factory.

The salt is washed and dried.

The salt is sorted.

Machines package
the salt.

People buy the salt.

Let's eat!

Picture Glossary

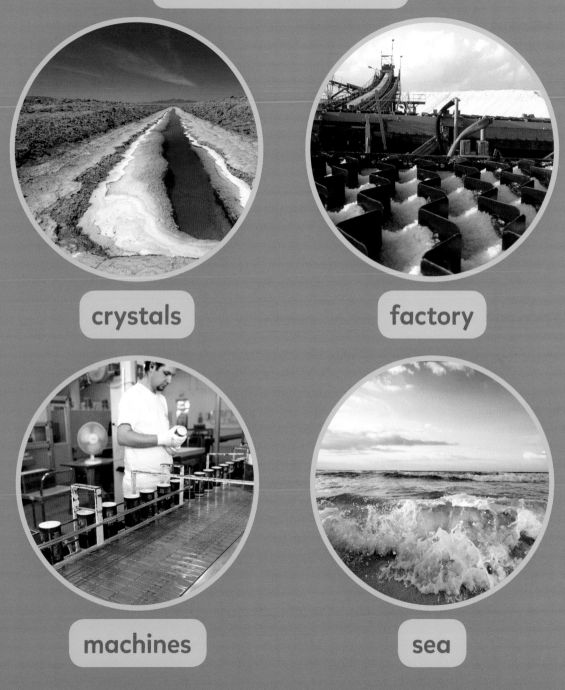

crystals

factory

machines

sea

Read More

Perish, Patrick. *Crystals*. Minneapolis: Bellwether Media, 2020.

Rivera, Andrea. *Minerals*. Minneapolis: Abdo, 2018.

Vilardi, Debbie. *Why Is the Ocean Salty?* Minneapolis: Pop!, 2019.

Index

crystal, 8

factory, 12

machine, 18

sea, 4

truck, 12

worker, 10